University of the State of New York
Extension Department
Albany, N. Y.

Syllabus 49   Dec. 1894

Subject no.
720.9

HISTORY OF ARCHITECTURAL STYLES

EVOLUTION, DEVELOPMENT AND RELATIONS OF THE HISTORIC TYPES

By A. D. F. Hamlin, M. A., Adjunct-Professor of Architecture, Columbia College, School of Mines

Lecture 1

INTRODUCTORY

Definitions

Architecture as an art. Engineering and building. Composition, motives, detail; scale and proportion; decoration and ornament. "Style" and "styles"; historic styles.

Architecture and civilization

Antiquity of building. Utility and beauty. Influence of material and intellectual advances. Architecture and religion. Influence of geographic, political and racial relations.

Evolution of styles

Growth *vs* creation. Paradox of primitive origins. Styles developed one out of another. Modifications and transformations. Archaism; perfection and decay. Persistence of types.

Criticism of style

Style and expression. Utility and beauty. Material and technic. Form and color. Symmetry and balance. The picturesque and the monumental.

General outline of historic relations

Primitive and prehistoric art. Egyptian, ancient oriental, Greek and Roman art. Early Christian and Byzantine art. Cathedral architecture. The renaissance. Oriental styles.

References

Fergusson. History of architecture.
——— History of modern styles of architecture.
Goodyear. History of art.
——— Roman and medieval art.
Lübke. Geschichte der architektur.
——— Outlines of the history of art.
Reber. History of ancient art.
——— History of medieval art.
Rosengarten. Handbook of architectural styles.
Viollet-le-Duc. Discourses on architecture.

Topics for papers

1 Relation of architecture to building, engineering and fine art.
2 Styles as exponents of civilization.

Lecture 2

EGYPTIAN AND ASSYRIAN STYLES

Periods in Egyptian art

Antiquity of Egyptian art. Sketch of the succession of kingdoms in the Nile valley. The Ramessidae, Ptolemaic and Roman periods.

General characteristics

Situation and climate. Religious beliefs and sepulchral art. Temples in general. Domestic and military architecture. Decorative art.

Sepulchral architecture

Successive types. The pyramid, mastaba and rock-cut tombs. Beni-hassan. Funereal sculpture. Painting and decoration.

Temple architecture

The plan. The pylons, courts, hypostyle hall, sekos. Types of piers and columns. Use of color and ornament. Important monuments.

Later architecture

Decadence and Ptolemaic revival. Changes in plan and style. Roman period.

Chaldean and Assyrian styles

Contrast to Egyptian art. Chaldean types. Assyrian palaces. Babylonian art. Question of the vault and column. Wall decoration. Relations to Egyptian, Persian and Ionian art.

References

Jomard. Recueil d'observations et de memoires sur l'Égypte ancienne et moderne.
Layard. Discoveries among the ruins of Nineveh and Babylon.
—— Nineveh and its remains.
Maspéro. Egyptian archæology.
Perrot *and* Chipiez. History of art in ancient Egypt.
—— History of art in Chaldæa and Assyria.
Place. Ninive et l'Assyrie.

See also References for Lecture 1

Topics for papers

1. Use of color and carving in Egyptian architecture.
2. Types of Egyptian temples.
3. Assyrian wall decoration.

Lecture 3

GREEK STYLES

Connecting links with Egyptian and oriental art
Assyria, Persia and Asia Minor. Phenician and Cypriote art. Prehistoric Greek art. Later relations with Egypt and the east.

The Doric temple
Theories as to Doric origins. The earlier temples. Doric temple in fifth century B. C. Analysis. Technic.

Principal monuments
In Magna Graecia. In Greece proper. The Theseum. The Parthenon. Decadence.

Ionic order
Meaning of the word "order." Origins of the Ionic. Analysis and technic. Chief monuments.

Corinthian order
A variant of the Ionic. Analysis and technic. Chief monuments. Alexandrine period.

Greek decoration
Sculpture and painting. Genesis of ornament-forms Polychromy. The Sidon sarcophagi.

Greco-Roman monuments

References

Collignon. Greek archæology.
Durm. Die Baukunst der Griechen.
Fergusson. History of architecture.
Gwilt. Encyclopædia of architecture.
Laloux. L' architecture grecque.
Lübke. Outlines of the history of art.
Reber. History of ancient art.

Rosengarten. Handbook of architectural styles.
Smith. Greek and Roman architecture.
Stuart *and* Revett. Antiquities of Athens.

Topics for papers
1 Buildings of the Athenian acropolis.
2 Doric and Ionic orders.
3 Greek ornament.

Lecture 4

ROMAN STYLES

Primitive Roman art
Race elements and character of Romans. Etruscans and their architecture. The arch and engineering.

Roman imperial architecture
Results of Grecian campaigns. Variety in Roman buildings. Vaulted construction and arcades. Roman planning. Characteristics resulting from organization of empire. Splendor and magnificence.

Roman orders
Adoption of Greek orders. Changes in their use and treatment. Analysis. Columnar and arched motives.

Decoration and ornament
Carving. Incrustation. Stucco-relief. Wall painting.

Domestic architecture
Palaces, villas, town dwellings. Pompeii.

References
Barozzi, da Vignola. Five orders of architecture.
Chambers. Civil architecture.
Durm. Die Baukunst der Etrusker. Die Baukunst der Römer.
Martha. Manuel d'archéologie étrusque et romaine.

Reber. History of ancient art.
Taylor *and* Cresy. Architectural antiquities of Rome.
Viollet-le-Duc. Discourses on architecture.

Topics for papers

1 Comparison of Greek and Roman orders.
2 Roman treatment of construction and decoration.
3 Pantheon and Colosseum.

Lecture 5

EARLY CHRISTIAN AND BYZANTINE STYLES

Early Christian architecture

Decadence of Roman art. The basilica made into a church. Treatment of the interior. Marble incrustation. Mosaic and fresco. Important monuments.

Byzantine architecture

Results of the founding of Constantinople. Asiatic, Greek and Roman elements. Development of oriental Christian art. Modification of Roman types.

Byzantine construction

Oriental vaulting. The pendentive dome. The church of St Sophia (so-called). Development of centralised design.

Byzantine decorations

Carving. Incrustation, mosaic and fresco. Scantiness of exterior decoration.

Monuments and schools

Byzantine style in Italy. In Russia and Armenia. In Greece. Relations with Celtic and Mohammedan art.

HISTORY OF ARCHITECTURAL STYLES

References

Bayet. L'art byzantin.
Fergusson. History of architecture.
Hübsch. Monuments de l'architecture chrétienne.
Lanciani. Pagan and Christian Rome.
Lethaby *and* Swainson. Church of Santa Sophia at Constantinople.
Lübke Outlines of the history of art.
Okely. Christian architecture in Italy.
Reber. History of medieval art.
Rosengarten. Handbook of architectural styles.
Salzenberg Alt-Christliche Baudenkmale von Constantinopel.
Texier *and* Pullan. Byzantine architecture.

Topics for papers

1 Byzantine domical architecture.
2 Color in Byzantine decoration.
3 St Sophia and St Mark's compared.

Lecture 6

MEDIEVAL STYLES

The church and architecture

The dark ages. Church, feudalism and state. Abbey, cathedral and parish church.

Development of cathedral type

Evolution from the basilica. Dominance of constructive considerations. Evolution of gothic vaulting. Stained glass and tracery. Carving and ornament.

Periods of Gothic architecture

Round-arched or Romanesque. Early pointed. Geometric or decorated. Flamboyant and perpendicular. Decadence.

French, English and German styles

Preeminence of French Gothic architecture. English plans. English vaulting. German Gothic art. Important monuments.

References
Babcock. Vaults.
Corroyer. L'architecture gothique.
Moore. Development and character of Gothic architecture.
Parker. A B C of Gothic architecture.
——— Introduction to Gothic architecture.
Reber. History of medieval art.
Van Rensselaer. English cathedrals.
Viollet-le-Duc. Architecture monastique (*see* his Dictionnaire raisonné de l'architecture, v. 1, p. 241–312).
——— Cathédrale (*see* his Dictionnaire raisonné de l'architecture, v. 2, p. 279–392).
——— Construction (*see* his Dictionnaire raisonné de l'architecture, v. 4, p. 1–279).

Topics for papers
1 English and French cathedrals.
2 Gothic vaulting.
3 Window tracery.

Lecture 7

MEDIEVAL AND RENAISSANCE STYLES

Local and national variations of the pointed styles
French leadership in constructive development. English cathedrals. French and English types contrasted. German Gothic. Spanish Gothic. Notable monuments.

Italian medieval architecture
Local schools and confusion of styles. The basilican, Italo-Byzantine, Lombard and Pisan round-arched styles. Pointed styles in Italy. Dominance of decorative ideals. Classic elements. Notable monuments.

Revival of learning
Decay of medievalism. Humanists. Precursors of the renaissance in art and literature. Study of classic models. Personal element.

HISTORY OF ARCHITECTURAL STYLES

References

Brandon. Analysis of Gothic architecture.
Palustre. L'architecture de la renaissance.
—— La renaissance en France.
Pater. The renaissance.
Rickman. Attempt to discriminate the styles of architecture.
Street. Gothic architecture of North Italy.
—— Some account of Gothic architecture in Spain.
Symonds. Renaissance in Italy; the fine arts.

See also References for Lecture 6.

Topics for papers

1 English and French cathedrals compared.
2 Gothic cathedrals of Italy.
3 Causes leading to the renaissance.

Lecture 8

RENAISSANCE STYLES

Renaissance in Italy

Early renaissance and its masters. Renaissance monuments in northern and central Italy. Palaces and churches. Transition and middle renaissance. Masters of the classic period. Palace-design in Rome, Venice, Vicenza and Genoa. Churches and domical design Decadence and later monuments. Decorative arts: fresco, carving, inlay, metal-work.

Renaissance in France

Its introduction from Italy. Period of the Valois kings. Chateaux and palaces. Churches. Middle renaissance; classicism Style from Louis 14 to the revolution; classic revival. The Louvre and Tuileries. Carving and ornament

Renaissance in the rest of Europe

In Spain: the three periods. Spanish decoration. Monuments. In Germany: characteristics. Castles and churches. In England: Elizabethan and Jacobean styles. Mansions, palaces and churches. Classic design in England; its masters and monuments. American colonial architecture.

References

Burckhardt. The Cicerone.
Gotch *and* Brown. Architecture of the renaissance in England.
Letarouilly. Édifices de Rome moderne.
Lübke. Geschichte der renaissance in Deutschland.
────── Geschichte der renaissance in Frankreich.
Müntz. La renaissance en Italie et en France.
Palustre. La renaissance en France.
Pattison. Renaissance of the fine arts in France.
Richardson. Architecture of Elizabeth and James.
Symonds. Renaissance in Italy: the fine arts.

See also general handbooks, previously referred to.

Topics for papers

1. Italian palaces.
2. St Peter's at Rome.
3. Early renaissance in France.
4. Domestic architecture of the renaissance in England.

Lecture 9

MOHAMMEDAN STYLES

Arabian architecture

Rise and conquests of Islam. Earlier mosques. Byzantine elements. Arcades, domes and minarets. Wall decoration. Saracenic or stalactite work. Geometric design. Moorish art in Spain. The Alhambra and other monuments.

Persian architecture

Persians, Aryans. Vaulted and domical construction. Decoration. Persian and Arabic art compared. Important monuments

Turkish architecture

Arabic and Persian elements. Conquest of Constantinople. Adoption of the Aya Sofia type for mosques. Variations and development of the type. Arcades, domes and minarets. Kiosques and fountains. Other monuments.

Indo-Moslem styles

Early Moslem art in India. Indian, Arabic and Persian elements. Mogul period. Chief centers and monuments. The Taj Mahal. Decoration.

References

Bourgoin. Les arts arabes.
Coste. Monuments modernes de la Perse.
Fergusson. History of architecture.
—— History of Indian and eastern architecture.
Franz-Pascha. Die Baukunst des Islam.
Jones. Plans, elevations and sections of the Alhambra.
Lübke. Geschichte der architektur.
—— Outlines of the history of art.
Parvillée. Architecture et décoration turques.
Prisse D'Avennes. L'art arabe.

Topics for papers

1 Arabian and Turkish mosques.
2 The Alhambra.

Lecture 10

MODERN STYLES

Classic and Gothic revivals

Art at close of last century. Greek revival in England. Roman revival in France. Victorian Gothic. French modern Gothic. German Greek revival. These revivals not permanent.

Confusion of styles

Modern archeology. *Ceci tuera cela.* Individualism. Changing requirements. Metallic construction. Styles in the United States. Commercial and ecclesiastical architecture.

Present tendencies

Variety in details not inconsistent with unity of tendency. Crystallization of a style. Lesson of the past. Renaissance styles and modern life. Paris, Berlin, Vienna. New York and Chicago. Cathedral of St John the Divine. The Columbian exposition. Conclusion.

Topics for papers

1 The Victorian Gothic.
2 Is a new architectural style in progress of development?
3 Analysis and criticism of one or more recent buildings of importance in the United States, preferably New York.

LIST OF AUTHORITIES REFERRED TO

Babcock. Vaults.

Barozzi, da Vignola, Giacomo. Five orders of architecture to which are added the Greek orders; ed. and tr. by A. L. Tuckerman. 12 p. 84 pl. sq. F. N. Y. 1891. Comstock. $5.

Bayet, Charles. L'art byzantin. Illus. O. Paris 1883. Quantin, 5 fr.

Bourgoin, Jules. Les arts arabes, architecture, menuiserie, bronzes, plafonds, revêtements, pavements, vitraux, etc. F. Paris 1868-70. Morel, 200 fr

Brandon, R. *and* J. A. Analysis of Gothic architecture. New ed. 2v. illus. Q Lond. 1873. Rimell, 63s.

Burckhardt, J. G. The Cicerone: art guide to painting in Italy. O. Lond 1879. Murray, 6s.

Chambers, *Sir* William. Decorative part of civil architecture. Illus. Q. Lond. 1883. Lockwood, 21s.

Collignon. Maxime. Greek archæology; tr. by J. H. Wright. Illus. O. Lond. 1886. Cassell, 5s. (Fine art lib.)

Corroyer, Édouard. L'architecture gothique. Illus. O. Paris 1891. Libraries imprimeries réunies, 50c. (Bibliothèque de l'enseignement des beaux-arts.)

Coste, Pascal. Monuments modernes de la Perse. Illus. F. Paris 1867. Morel, 160 fr.

Durm, Joseph. Die Baukunst der Etrusker. Die Baukunst der Römer. 368 p. illus. O. Darmstadt 1885. Deihl, 20m. (Handbuch der architektur.)

—— Die Baukunst der Griechen. Ed. 2. 386p. illus. O. Darmstadt 1892. Bergsträsser, 20m. (Handbuch der architektur.)

Fergusson, James. History of architecture in all countries from the earliest times to the present day. 2v. illus. O. N. Y. Dodd, $7.50.
Best general history of architecture in English

—— History of Indian and eastern architecture. New ed. 2v. illus. O. N. Y. 1891. Dodd, $10.

—— History of the modern styles of architecture. 2v. illus. O. N. Y. 1891. Dodd, $10.

Franz-Pascha, Julius. Die Baukunst des Islam. 150p. illus. O. Darmstadt, 1887. Diehl, 11m. (Handbuch der architektur.)

Goodyear, W: H. History of art. Illus O. N. Y. 1888. Barnes, $3.

—— Roman and medieval art. (Chautauqua reading course.)

Gotch, J. A. and Brown, W. T. Architecture of the renaissance in England. 6 pts. illus. F. Bost. 1893. Ticknor, $8 per pt pap.

Gwilt, Joseph. Encyclopædia of architecture. 1459 p. illus. O. N. Y. 1888. Longmans, $17.50.

Hübsch, Henri. Monuments de l'architecture chrétienne. F. Paris 1866. Morel, 150 fr.

Jomard, E. F. Recueil d'observations et de memoires sur l'Égypte ancienne et moderne. 4v. O. Paris 1830.

Jones, Owen. Plans, elevations and sections of the Alhambra. 2v. illus F. Lond. 1842-45. £12. *Out of print.*

Laloux, Victor. L'architecture grecque. O. Paris 1888. Quantin, 3 fr. 50c.
To be read with caution as it contains a number of inaccuracies of detail; otherwise a handy manual.

Lanciani, Rodolfo. Pagan and Christian Rome. Illus. O. Bost. Houghton, $6.

Layard, *Sir* A. H: Discoveries among the ruins of Nineveh and Babylon; with travels in Armenia, Kurdistan and the desert, a second expedition for the British museum. Ed. 2. D. N. Y. 1875. Barnes, $1.75.

—— Nineveh and its remains and an inquiry into the manners and arts of the ancient Assyrians. D. N. Y. 1852. Putnam. $1.

Letarouilly, P. M. Édifices de Rome moderne. 3 v. Q. and atlas 3 v. F. Paris 1840-57 Bance, 390 fr.
Lethaby, W. R. *and* Swainson, H. Church of Sancta Sophia at Constantinople, a study of Byzantine building. O. N. Y. 1894. Macmillan, $6.50.
Lübke, Wilhelm. Geschichte der architektur von den ältesten zeiten bis auf die gegenwart dargestellt. Ed. 6. 2 v. O. Leipzig 1885. Seemann, 26 m.
—— Geschichte der renaissance in Deutschland. Ed. 2. 2 v. O. Stuttgart 1881-82. Ebner & Seubert, 28 m.
—— Geschichte der renaissance in Frankreich. Ed 2. O. Leipzig 1885. Ebner & Seubert, 17 m.
—— Outlines of the history of art. 2 v. O. N. Y. 1891. Dodd, $7.50.
Martha, Jules. Manuel d'archéologie étrusque et romaine. Illus. O. Paris 1884. Quantin, 3 fr. 50 c. (Bibliothèque de l'enseignement des beaux-arts.)
Maspéro, G. Egyptian archæology; from the French by A. B. Edwards. Illus. O. N. Y. 1887. Putnam, $3.
Moore, C: H. Development and character of Gothic architecture. Illus. O. N. Y. 1890. Macmillan, $4 50.
Müntz, Eugènie. La renaissance en Italie et en France à l'epoque de Charles 8. Illus. Q. Paris 1885. Didot, 30 fr.
Okely, W. S. Development of Christian architecture in Italy. Illus. O. Lond. 1860. Longmans, 14 s.
Palustre Léon. L'architecture de la renaissance. Illus. O. Paris 1892. May & Motteroz, 3 fr. 50 c. (Bibliothèque de l'enseignement des beaux-arts.)
—— La renaissance en France. 2 v. F. Paris 1879-83. Quantin, 250 fr.
Parker, J: H: A B C of Gothic architecture. Ed. 6. Illus. S. N. Y. 1888. Little, Brown & Co $1.25.
—— Introduction to Gothic architecture. Ed. 7. Illus. S. N. Y. 1888. Little, Brown & Co $2.
Parvillée, Léon. Architecture et décoration turques au 15° siècle. F. Paris, 1874. Morel, 120 fr.
Pater, Walter. The renaissance: studies in art and literature. O. Lond. 1888. Macmillan, 10s. 6d.
Pattison, *Mrs* Mark. Renaissance of the fine arts in France. 2 v illus. O. N Y. 1879. Dodd, $7.50.
Perrot, Georges *and* Chipiez, Charles. History of art in ancient Egypt; tr. and ed. by W. Armstrong. 2 v. illus. O N. Y. 1884. Armstrong, $15.50.

Perrot, Georges *and* Chipiez, Charles. History of art in Chaldæa and Assyria. 2 v illus. O. N. Y 1885. Armstrong, $15.50.
Place, Victor. Ninive et l'Assyrie. 3. v. F. Paris 1866-69. Baudry, 850 fr. (Imprimerie impériale.)
Prisse D'Avennes. L'art arabe d'après les monuments du kaire depuis le 7⁰ siècle jusqu' à la fin du 17⁰. IV. Q & atlas. Paris 1869-77 Morel, grande ed. 1050 fr.; petite ed. 650 fr.
Reber, Franz von. History of ancient art. Illus. O. N. Y. 1882 Harper, $3.50.
—— History of mediæval art. Illus. O. N. Y. 1887. Harper, $5.
Richardson, C. J. Architecture of Elizabeth and James 1. F. Lond., 1840. Maclean, 84s.
Rickman, Thomas. Attempt to discriminate styles of architecture in England. Ed. 7. O. Lond. 1881. Parker 16s.
Rosengarten, Albert. Handbook of architectural styles; tr. by W. Collett-Sanders. Illus. O. Lond. 1888. Chatto, 7s. 6d.
Salzenberg, W. Alt-Christliche baudenkmale von Constantinopel von 5 bis 12 jahrhundert. F. Berlin 1854. Ernst & Korn, 60m.
Smith, T: R. Greek and Roman architecture. O. Lond. Chapman. (South Kensington museum. Science and art handbooks.)
Street, G: E. Gothic architecture of North Italy. O. Lond. 1874. Murray, 26s.
—— Some account of Gothic architecture in Spain. Ed. 2. O. Lond. 1869. Murray, 30s.
Stuart, James *and* Revett, Nicholas. Antiquities of Athens and other monuments of Greece. Illus. D. Lond. 1889. Bell, $1.50. (Bohn's illustrated lib.)
Symonds, J. A. Renaissance in Italy. New ed. 5 v. O. N. Y. 1885. Holt, $10.
Taylor, G. L. *and* Cresy, Edward. Architectural antiquities of Rome. New ed. Illus. F. Lond 1874. Lockwood, 63s.
Texier, C. *and* Pullan, R. P. Byzantine architecture. F. Lond. 1865. Day, 126s.
Van Rensselaer, *Mrs* Schuyler. English cathedrals. 395 p. illus. O. N. Y. 1892. Century co., $6.
Viollet-le-Duc, E. E. Dictionnaire raisonné de l'architecture française du 11⁰ au 16⁰ siècle, 10 v. illus. O. Paris 1875. Morel, 250 fr.
—— Discourses on architecture; from the French by B: Bucknall. New ed. 2 v. illus. O. Bost. 1889. Ticknor, $15. *Out of print.*

Lightning Source UK Ltd.
Milton Keynes UK
UKHW020656210322
400379UK00004B/52